34880000823851

BOOK CHARGING CARD

973.9
CRA

Accession No. _____ Call No. _____

Author *Craats, Rennay*

Title *History of the 1900's*

973.9
CRA

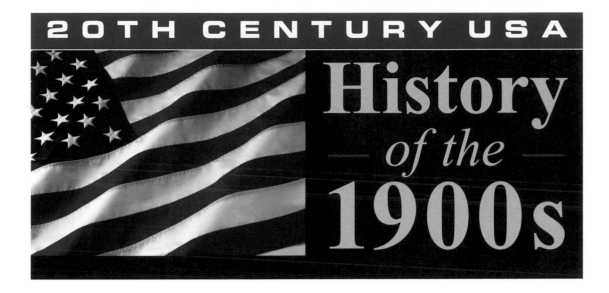

20TH CENTURY USA

History of the 1900s

Rennay Craats

WEIGL PUBLISHERS INC.

Published by Weigl Publishers Inc.
123 South Broad Street
Mankato, MN, USA   56002
Web site: http://www.weigl.com

Library of Congress Cataloging-in-Publication Data available upon request
from the publisher. Fax (507) 388-2746 for the attention of the Publishing
Records Department.

ISBN 1-930954-42-5

Printed and bound in the United States of America
1 2 3 4 5 6 7 8 9 0   05 04 03 02 01

Senior Editor
Jared Keen

Series Editor
Carlotta Lemieux

Copy Editor
Heather Kissock

Layout and Design
Warren Clark
Carla Pelky

Photo Research
Angela Lowen
Joe Nelson

Photograph Credits
Archive Photos: pages 20, 26, 42; Bettmann/CORBIS: pages 15, 29, 43; Digital Stock: page 14;
George Eastman House/Lewis W. Hine/Archive Photos: page 39; Historic Photo Archive/Archive
Photos: page 22; Hulton/Archive: pages 3MR, 6R, 7L, 18, 19, 21, 24, 28, 31, 35, 36, 37, 38, 40;
Museum of the City of New York/Archive Photos: page 11, 34; National Archives of Canada:
page 30; Photofest: pages 3TL, 3BL, 6L, 7R, 10, 12, 16, 17, 23, 25, 27, 32, 33, 41; Reuters
NewMedia Inc./CORBIS: page 8; Visuals Unlimited: pages 9, 13.

USA 1900s Contents

Edison Takes Control

Nobel Prizes

The Great Fire

RAGTIME

Picasso's Cubes

Football Fatalities

Stock Scares

Boer War is Over

Texas Floods

Anti-Saloon Movement

The beginning of the new century was an exciting period for the U.S. It was a time of firsts. It was in the 1900s that the first airplane took flight in North Carolina. It was the first time a radio message was sent overseas or an automobile was driven across the country. This decade marked the first World Series championship, the first time a motion picture spliced scenes together through editing, and the first time iced tea and ice cream cones were enjoyed. The 1900s was also a decade of terrible firsts. It was the first time the U.S. participated in **guerrilla** warfare in Southeast Asia and the first time an earthquake rocked a major city on the country's West Coast.

20th Century USA: History of the 1900s explores these firsts as well as many other important events and people of the day. These pages follow the leadership of President Theodore Roosevelt after the assassination of President McKinley and tell of

Hello, Jell-O

Kodak Moments

World's Fair

North Pole Reached

Olympic Triumphs

Asian Restrictions

Wizard of Oz

PRESIDENT DEAD

Peter Pan

oil booms, bank busts, and the development of the automobile. Americans in the 1900s cheered on sports heroes such as Cy Young, May Sutton, and Jack Johnson. They paid money to watch nickelodeon presentations of their favorite **vaudeville** and film stars, and they took snapshots with ease.

20th Century USA: History of the 1900s presents a selection of the many noteworthy happenings from this time. If you see a story that interests you, visit your local library to read old newspapers and magazines preserved on microfilm. The Internet, encyclopedias, and other reference books are great research tools to learn more about this fascinating decade. For now, turn the page and journey back to the turn of the century.

USA 1900s Time Line

1900
The U.S. says "aloha" to Hawai'i. The area becomes an official U.S. territory. Read more on page 20.

1900
The U.S. Army battles the bug. The mosquito experiments, conducted by army doctors, save lives. Find out how on page 26.

1900
Galveston, Texas, is under the weather. Read about the hurricane that nearly destroyed the town on page 8.

1900
Americans say cheese. The Brownie allows people to take their own snapshots. Page 14 has more about this popular point-and-click arrival.

1901
After sixty-four years at the helm, Queen Victoria dies. Britain mourns its monarch but welcomes a new-style leader. To read more about King Edward VII, turn to page 16.

1902
Britain and the Dutch Boers end their war in South Africa. Find out what caused the conflict on page 18.

1902
President Roosevelt has no trust in trusts. He flexes his political muscles at the Northern Securities Company. See what happened on page 22.

1903
Construction begins on a chocolate factory in Derry Church, Pennsylvania. Find out what became of its owner and the town on page 15.

1903
Wilbur and Orville Wright are soaring the skies. Their airplane designs are a success. Learn more about this revolutionary invention on page 27.

1903
Jack London's adventures are a hit. *The Call of the Wild* becomes a classic adventure tale. Find out more about this talented author on page 25.

1904
The ice-cream cone makes its debut at the St. Louis World's Fair. Turn to page 11 to discover what else was brewing at this historic event.

1904
New York City's population heads underground. The subway system is incredible. Read more about this new mode of transportation on page 27.

1904
U.S. sound takes back Broadway. George Cohan produces a truly American musical. Turn to page 41 to read more about this talented composer.

1904
President Roosevelt is voted in. Page 23 has the election coverage.

King Edward VII

President Roosevelt

1904

Russia and Japan butt heads over territory. The resulting war is a bloody one. Find out the details on page 19.

1905

People are afraid of too much immigration. They turn their fears against the Asian community. Turn to page 38 to find out about the Asiatic Exclusion League and what it meant for future Asian Americans.

1905

May Sutton owns the court at Wimbledon. She is the first U.S. athlete to win the tournament. Read about this tennis player's great success on page 31.

1905

A group of African Americans meets to discuss civil rights and politics. Learn how this improves the nation on page 33.

1906

San Francisco shakes! The earthquake causes damage and sets fires that sweep through the city. Turn to page 9 to find out more about the disaster.

1906

The president is congratulated for making peace. He is given the world's most prestigious award. Find out what he wins and why on page 23.

1906

Upton Sinclair exposes America to the jungle. His novel causes quite a stir. Turn to page 24 to read about this book's impact on society.

1907

Another state joins the Union. Discover how it becomes part of the U.S. on page 21.

1907

The circus is in town—and it is not the usual production. Learn more about this super-circus on page 13.

1907

The banks come tumbling down. The economic panic is eased by some quick action. Page 35 tells how the crisis was handled.

1907

Nickelodeons arrive in stores across the country. This inexpensive form of entertainment is a big hit. Find out more on page 13.

1907

Fashion relaxes. S-shape dresses give way to a more comfortable style. Page 36 has the details.

1908

President Roosevelt tries to save the land. He establishes the Congress of Governors to help in his efforts. Page 21 has more.

1909

Robert Peary is on top of the world. Read about the explorer's accomplishment on page 16.

1909

The union helps women garment workers. Find out how strikes make things better for the members of the International Ladies' Garment Workers Union on page 34.

May Sutton

Ringling Brothers and Barnum & Bailey Circus

Floods Soak Texas

Galveston, Texas, was the nation's fastest growing port at the turn of the century. Money flowed into the area, and no one stopped to worry about what else could flood it.

The city had been built on a sandbar only about 9 feet above sea level. In the autumn of 1900, the town heard about a tropical storm brewing in the Caribbean. By September 7, the temperature had dropped, and waves were crashing on the shore. The next morning, the wind speed rose to about 50 miles an hour, and water poured through the streets. Within hours, the winds became a hurricane. The electricity was knocked out, plunging the city into darkness. The only bridge to the mainland collapsed, trapping residents in the storm. Many crowded into the tallest hotel in the middle of town, hoping to escape the flood's reach.

■ The Galveston hurricane nearly wiped the town off the map, killing almost 8,000 people.

By evening, rain and seawater were flooding the streets—and the water level was still rising. Houses that had been ripped from the ground drifted in the waves. Several people floated on makeshift rafts of timber, waiting for the storm to die down or for someone to help them. Finally, around midnight, the winds slowed, and the rain stopped. Nearly 3,000 homes (about half the residential area of Galveston) had been swept into the sea and thousands lost their lives. It took several months for residents and emergency workers to clean up the city.

THEATER FIRE

■ On December 30, 1903, about 1,900 people gathered at the splendid Iroquois Theater in Chicago, Illinois. Because the theater was thought to be fireproof, the management had not followed standard fire precautions, such as having firefighters on hand and pikes to pull scenery down. Most theater fires resulted from hot lights that came in contact with scenery. The disaster at the Iroquois Theater was no exception.

At 3:15 PM, a hot light set fire to a velvet curtain. The flames spread quickly. The asbestos blanket that was supposed to block the audience from a stage fire became stuck. People panicked and rushed toward the exits to escape the flames, but many of the doors were locked or opened inward. About 600 people died in the accident. Many victims were crushed by the stampede of people desperate for a way out. It was the worst single-building fire in U.S. history. The disaster prompted many cities throughout the country to improve their fire policies for public buildings.

The Great Fire

San Franciscans were shaken awake on April 19, 1906, at 5:12 AM by a violent earthquake. In some areas, the land along the San Andreas Fault shifted as much as 21 feet. Many buildings crumpled under the pressure, but this was not the worst of the disaster. Water, gas, and electrical lines broke. The fire that resulted spread quickly through town, eating up everything in its path. That evening, thousands of residents fled to Oakland and Berkeley across the bay. From there, they watched their city burn. Several landmarks, including the San Francisco Call building, were destroyed.

By the time the fire finally burned itself out, it had destroyed more than 75 percent of San Francisco. About 38,000 buildings were lost, 300,000 people were homeless, and damages and property losses were estimated at $400 million. There was also heavy loss of life. At least 315 people had been killed instantly, 352 were missing and assumed dead, 6 people had been shot for crimes during the disaster, and another person had been shot accidentally.

■ Measuring 8.25 on the Richter scale, the San Francisco earthquake and fire is considered to be one of the worst natural disasters in U.S. history.

Senseless Sea Disaster

The *General Slocum* offered pleasure cruises around the New York harbor. On June 15, 1904, about 1,360 people climbed aboard. A fire was discovered on the ship, but the captain did not react. Passing ships blasted their whistles to alert the ship of danger. The *General Slocum* kept on course. Firefighters, with extinguishers ready, waited for the ship to pull toward the pier. Smoke and flames spread, and people leaped into the river to get away from the intense heat. The captain, finally realizing the size of the problem, attempted to pull ashore. He misjudged the distance and crashed into rocks. Passengers tried to free lifeboats, but the boats were wired in place. Others tried to jump overboard, but the ship's side-paddles continued to rotate and injured many people. The life preservers were filled with sawdust and metal rather than with the more expensive cork. Those who wore them sank like stones. Other ships rescued a few passengers once the *General Slocum* was grounded. As close as the ship was to shore, 1,031 people died. The captain survived the disaster and was sentenced to ten years in prison for negligence causing death.

Blockbuster Barrymore

Ethel Barrymore came from a talented family. Both of her parents were successful actors, and so were her brothers John and Lionel. Barrymore was hailed as an amazing young actress for her role in the 1901 production of *Captain Jinks of the Horse Marines*. It was her first starring role on Broadway. She continued her winning streak with lead roles in *A Doll's House* in 1905 and *Alice-Sit-by-the-Fire* the following year. By this time, she had become one of the most sought-after actors in U.S. theater. Her unique style and sense of humor made audiences adore her for more than forty years. Her love of acting inspired her to establish the Ethel Barrymore Theater in New York City in 1928. Throughout her career, she performed in Shakespearean and other plays, appeared in movies, and wrote her autobiography, simply titled *Memories* (1955).

Porter a Pioneer

Edwin S. Porter contributed much to the entertainment industry of the decade. He was one of the first filmmakers to use closeups and other techniques to help get the story across in silent movies. This projectionist, inventor, and entrepreneur began his career with the Edison company in 1900, where he became the head of film production.

By the following year, he was blazing a trail in creative filmmaking with such films as *The Execution of Czolgosz*—the story of the execution of President McKinley's assassin. In it, he combined actual footage of the prison with actors portraying the drama that unfolded.

Porter had an unbeatable eye for detail and for spotting talent. He gave an unknown actor and playwright a role in his 1907 production *Rescued From an Eagle's Nest*. This unknown was D. W. Griffith, who went on to become one of the greatest directors ever and earned the title "Father of the Motion Picture." Porter explored filmmaking through Rex Films, his own company, which he established in 1911. He then worked for Famous Players. Porter continued producing films, although none was as spectacular as his earlier achievements.

Buster Brown Hits the Strips

In 1902, the *New York Herald* welcomed Buster Brown and his dog, Tige, to the funny pages. The cartoonist, R. F. Outcault, was no stranger to successful comic strips. His was the first U.S. cartoon set up as a strip in 1895. Its main character, a street **ragamuffin**, wore a long, dirty nightshirt. The printers of this strip experimented with yellow ink, and they tried it out on the nightshirt. This earned the strip its name, "The Yellow Kid." With his Buster Brown strip, Outcault continued to prove that comics could sell newspapers. In the strip, he created a winning combination of harmless mischief and strong moral messages. Millions of young Americans were glued to the adventures of Buster Brown. It was one of the most popular cartoons in the papers.

Fantasy Role

Scottish writer J. M. Barrie was excited about his new children's play, *Peter Pan*. It was based on stories he had told to a group of brothers in London. Barrie approached U.S. actress Maude Adams to star in the production in 1904. At first, he wanted her to play several roles in *Peter Pan*. Then, within a year, the play opened in New York with Adams appearing as the title character. The critics and audiences adored her, insisting that she was made for the part. She was Peter Pan until 1907. Adams retired at the height of her stage career after appearing in Edmond Rostand's *Chantecler* in 1911. Although she had retired, she continued to appear as the boy who never grows up in *Peter Pan* revivals for twenty years. During that time, she performed in front of more than 2 million people. Despite her other triumphs, she was always associated with her most popular role—Peter Pan.

■ J. M. Barrie's most famous work, *Peter Pan*, has been made into a silent movie, musical comedy, and full-length feature cartoon.

EVERYBODY LOVES A FAIR

■ In 1904, the St. Louis World's Fair finally opened its gates—a year later than expected. The fair was intended to celebrate the centennial of the Louisiana Purchase. Instead, it became a celebration of life in a new time. While people wandered from exhibit to exhibit, they could enjoy several new treats— hamburgers, iced tea, and ice-cream cones—from fair vendors. A concession stand owner noticed that his hot tea sales were slow. He put ice in the beverage and offered fair-goers a way to beat the heat. Iced tea was a hit. As well, ice-cream vendors created edible ice-cream holders to cut down on waste and save money on dishes. Americans have been enjoying cones ever since.

Ziegfeld's Follies

Florenz Ziegfeld grew up in Chicago, Illinois, where he managed vaudeville tours around the world. After marrying actress Anna Held, Ziegfeld created seven musicals in which she starred, including *Papa's Wife* (1899) and *Miss Innocence* (1908). He also produced musical theater productions, such as *Show Boat* (1927) and *Bitter Sweet* (1929). Ziegfeld became famous for introducing **revues** to the country's musical stage. One such revue, beginning in New York City in 1907, included twenty-one "follies."

The revues became known as Ziegfeld's Follies. The follies featured chorus girls, the best actors of the day, and incredibly elaborate sets. Through the years, Zigfield's Follies were a launching pad for many famous singers and comedians, including W. C. Fields, Billie Burke, Fanny Brice, Eddie Cantor, and Will Rogers. Each year, a new follies production was offered until Ziegfeld's death in 1932.

■ The chorus girls of Ziegfeld's Follies thrilled audiences with their high skirts and flowered bonnets.

RUSSIAN STAR

■ Alla Nazimova emigrated from Russia to the U.S. in 1905. At first she appeared in plays produced in Russian. Then the talented actress set out to learn English so that she could work in the mainstream. It did not take long. After six months of English lessons, Nazimova was ready to take Hollywood by storm. She appeared in her first English movie in 1906—*Hedda Gabler* by the Norwegian dramatist Henrik Ibsen. Nazimova's passionate portrayal and exotic style made her a success. During her career, she received praise for performances in such stage productions as *The Cherry Orchard* (1928) and *Mourning Becomes Electra* (1931) and movies including *Camille* (1921), *A Doll's House* (1922), and *The Bridge of San Luis Rey* (1944). Nazimova continued working on the stage and in movies until her death in 1945.

Cartoon Movement

Flipping pictures quickly, one to the next, creates the illusion of movement. This fact became valuable in 1906, when J. Stuart Blackton used this idea to create the first motion picture cartoon. He collected a series of photographed drawings and showed them in quick succession to make what appeared to be continuous motion. His experimental cartoon was called *Humorous Phases of Funny Faces*. The sketched face blew cigar smoke at a woman's face, making her disappear behind the cloud. Following this, the person in the picture seemed to draw himself and then tip his hat to the camera to end his performance. While Blackton's work was rough, it paved the way for more sophisticated cartoonists, such as Emile Cohl of France and Winsor McCay from the U.S.

Clowning Around

There was nothing like the circus for quality entertainment. Dozens of circuses toured the U.S. in the 1900s, but two stood above the rest—the Barnum & Bailey circus and the Ringling Brothers circus were unbeatable. The Ringling Brothers had taken over many smaller circuses. In 1905, the Ringlings bought 50 percent of James Bailey's shares in the Barnum & Bailey circus. After Bailey's death in 1906, they bought the remaining 50 percent from his widow for $100,000. Two years of negotiations and $400,000 later, the Ringling Brothers finally purchased their major competitor—Barnum & Bailey Circus—on July 8, 1907. The two circuses traveled separately at first, but in 1919, the Ringlings brought them together to create a super-circus. This formed the Ringling Bros. and Barnum & Bailey Combined Shows. The new circus made its debut in New York City's Madison Square Garden. It required 100 double-length railroad cars and 1,200 employees to keep the operation running. It was the most glitzy show-business presentation to date, and it earned its slogan "The Greatest Show on Earth."

■ The Ringling Brothers and Barnum & Bailey Circus is the oldest entertainment attraction in the U.S.

EDISON TAKES CONTROL

■ Thomas Edison's New York company had created the first film studio in 1893. He also controlled much of the film equipment through registering **patents**. By 1900, many other filmmakers were using equipment based on Edison's designs. Edison sued them all. Many small studios could not afford the legal fees, so they folded. To those who Edison could not eliminate right away, he proposed a deal. He suggested that they bring all their patented goods together to form a holding company. If this trust was established, Edison promised to drop the lawsuits. In December 1908, the Motion Picture Patents Company was born. Most of the company's shares were owned by Edison and his former rival studio, the Biograph Company. Anyone wanting to make a movie in the U.S. had to pay a fee to the company. Some filmmakers fought against the trust. They made movies in secret, despite legal bullying. Many of them moved to Los Angeles to get away from the trust's reach. Hollywood became the movie center of the country. Edison's company controlled the movie industry until 1915, when the trust was dissolved under the Sherman Antitrust Act.

Plugging the Nickelodeon

For a nickel, Americans could enjoy quality entertainment. Storefronts in cities and towns were converted into theaters, with colorful posters advertising the current show. A screen and a piano stood in front of rows of chairs to turn a storeroom into a theater. Audiences paid their money to watch the ten-minute features, which were most often vaudeville acts. The nickelodeon, named for the admission price, sometimes also showed scenes from films. An "illustrated song" performed by a solo vocalist followed the presentation. This inexpensive form of entertainment brought in Americans across the country.

Point and Click

In 1900, the Eastman Kodak Company announced, "You press the button, we do the rest." The new box camera called the Brownie made photography available to a wider group of people. It was small and easy to use, which the company hoped would appeal to young Americans. With the simplicity and fun of the Brownie, even children could now take pictures. At the cost of $1, the Brownie gave the user good-quality photographs without having to focus or time the exposure. To sweeten the appeal, Kodak said it would develop the film so amateurs would not have to battle with the mysteries of darkrooms. This marked the emergence of the shapshot.

◼ With the Brownie came the promise of film processing. Photographers no longer had to develop their own photos.

WHAT'S NEW?

◼ The 1900s brought with it many new products and inventions. Here are some of the decade's innovations:

1900 – Firestone tires

1901 – instant coffee

1902 – Jell-O

1903 – license plates

1904 – tea bags

1905 – Vick's VapoRub (marketed as Vick's Magic Croup Salve)

1906 – electric washing machine

1907 – L'Oréal perfume and beauty products

1908 – Dixie Cup paper cups

1909 – electric toasters

Pedal Power

The invention of the modern bicycle caused a buzz around the world. It was an inexpensive form of transportation and a great way to get exercise. Doctors relied on bicycles to do their house calls. Boys working for telegraph companies raced through the streets on their bicycles to deliver messages. The bicycle also changed the way people lived. Automobiles were just a fantasy for most Americans, but bicycles made it easy for them to get around. Employees could now live farther from the hustle and bustle of the inner city. They traveled to work and back on their bicycles. Cycling through the country became a weekend vacation idea. Families enjoyed the freedom offered by these new vehicles.

Slang

skidoo
make a quick getaway

drool
nonsense

muckraker
a person who is interested in "raking the filth" to expose issues

jitney
a nickel

eye
a private investigator

humdinger
great

scuttlebutt
a rumor

Little Doll

Rose O'Neill was well known for her drawings of adorable chubby angels with pointed heads. This talent led to an international sensation. In 1909, she made her art **three-dimensional** with the Kewpie doll. It was one of the first character dolls—those based on a real person or personality—in the U.S. Originally, the dolls were made of **celluloid**. Little girls around the globe loved their Kewpie dolls. The demand was incredible, and the public insisted on more Kewpie dolls. These darlings were soon made from many materials, from **bisque** to chocolate. At one time, there were thirty-six factories in Germany devoted to producing bisque Kewpie dolls. To meet society's need for all things Kewpie, other products were soon released. Kewpie greeting cards, tableware, and jewelry flew off the shelves. This fad remained strong for nearly twenty years. It also served Rose O'Neill well. She earned more than $2 million in royalties from companies creating Kewpie products. Her popularity spread from dolls to other areas. O'Neill also wrote four novels, several short stories, a collection of poetry, and many children's books. She illustrated all these works with her own drawings. She was one of the most popular and in-demand magazine illustrators—not to mention the highest paid female illustrator—in the country.

Sweet Tooth

Milton Snavely Hershey began his career in chocolate in 1893. He bought a German chocolate-making machine and started producing chocolate-covered caramels. The next year, he created the Hershey Chocolate Company to make cocoa, baker's chocolate, and sweet chocolate. Later, he sold the caramel business for $1 million and focused solely on chocolate. In 1903, Hershey began the two-year construction of a new chocolate factory in his hometown of Derry Church, Pennsylvania. He had promised people chocolate, he said, and chocolate they would get! He had a vision of quality chocolate available for everyday Americans at a reasonable price. Chocolate-making became such a huge part of Derry Church that the town was renamed Hershey. Before long, Hershey was producing more milk chocolate than any other place in the world.

■ Milton Hershey's company has been making chocolate for more than 100 years.

Heading North

On April 6, 1909, U.S. explorer Robert Peary teetered on the top of the world. He was the first person to reach the North Pole. This accomplishment was a lifelong dream for Peary, and the expedition had been long and difficult. The team of 6 Americans, 17 Inuit, 19 sleds, and 133 sled dogs left on March 1. By the time they neared the Pole, the group was much smaller. For the last leg of the trip, Peary took with him only four Inuit and Matthew Henson, an African American. In temperatures of −15° Fahrenheit— mild in the Arctic— Peary planted a U.S. flag and claimed the area for the president. The explorers were photographed at the North Pole and then began their journey home. In September, Peary announced his achievement. There was instant controversy as U.S. explorer Dr. Frederick Cook claimed to have beaten the team there. After experts examined the claims, they established that Cook's was false. Peary's record was accepted. Peary was later given the rank of rear admiral for his accomplishments, and he retired in 1911.

Hail, the King of England

After sixty-four years as Britain's beloved monarch, Queen Victoria died on January 22, 1901. She had sat on the throne for longer than any other British monarch in history. During her reign, the British Empire had grown enormously, spreading across much of the world. Her successor and son, Edward VII, brought new freedom and modernization to the monarchy. Victoria had been very proper. Edward breathed vitality and fun into the country. His casual, real-world personality endeared Edward to his subjects. They celebrated his rule until his death in 1910. In his short time as King of England, the framework was set for the modern constitutional monarchy.

■ **Edward VII promoted friendship and peace among European nations.**

FIRST NOBEL PRIZE WINNERS

Chemistry	Jacobus H. Van't Hoff (Netherlands)
Literature	R. F. A. Sully-Prudhomme (France)
Peace	Jean Henri Dunant (Switzerland) Frédéric Passy (France)
Physics	Wilhelm C. Roentgen (Germany)
Physiology or Medicine	Emil Adolph von Behring (Germany)

Picasso's Cubes

Spain's Pablo Picasso saw art differently from many of his contemporaries. His 1907 painting *Les Demoiselles d'Avignon* showed just how different his vision was. Instead of painting a lifelike portrait, Picasso used fragments of the body. This new style was called cubism. Picasso and others who had embraced this form of art looked to get at the "truth" of a person or object by breaking it into parts. Traditional artists used shadow, perspective, and light to reveal their subject, but cubists presented their subjects using geometric shapes. Subjects in cubist paintings would often have disproportioned body parts, such as one huge ear or three tiny fingers.

Rewarding Good Work

Alfred Nobel was a successful and wealthy industrialist. He was also interested in the arts and science. Although he had invented dynamite, he was a strong **pacifist**. A newspaper printed that Nobel was dead and called him the "merchant of death" in the obituary. The very alive Nobel did not want to be remembered that way. He was determined to leave a legacy of peace once he was gone. When the Swedish millionaire died in 1896, his will shocked his family. Most of his fortune was to be placed into a fund to provide prizes. Every year, five people around the world who had benefited humankind through their achievements in chemistry, physics, medicine, literature, and peacemaking, were to be granted

■ Alfred Nobel was a great inventor. He held more than 350 patents and owned companies and laboratories in more than 20 countries.

a prize. Nobel specified that a person's nationality did not matter—the best person in that field would receive the prize. He also designated organizations that would choose the winners.

Nobel's will was not clearly worded, and his family spent five years fighting over the money. The first Nobel Prizes were finally awarded on December 10, 1901. Each winner received the astounding sum of $42,000—an award dozens of times larger than any other at the time. Today, the prize, which also includes achievement in economics, is nearly $1 million. It is the most prestigious award in the world.

St. Pierre Disaster

St. Pierre was the largest and most prosperous town on the island of Martinique in the French West Indies. On May 8, 1902, many people in St. Pierre were on their way to church when Montagne Pelée, the volcano that stood 4,583 feet over their city, erupted. In a matter of minutes, a river of scalding lava buried the town. Smoke and ash rose 7 miles in the air over St. Pierre. Ash fell as far away as Jamaica, and Barbados was buried in 2 million tons of it. St. Pierre was home to many rum distilleries, which were destroyed. To make matters worse, the alcohol caught fire in the incredible heat. The harbor was engulfed in flames when a **tsunami** washed over it. Thousands were killed instantly. Of the town's 30,000 residents, only one man in a jail cell lived through the eruption.

St. Pierre was not the only town to suffer the fury of Montagne Pelée. Many smaller towns around it were wiped out as well. A few hours after the eruption, the volcanic activity set off another volcano on the island of St. Vincent. This eruption killed hundreds as molten rock and ash spewed from the mountain. The U.S. and Europe launched a relief effort, but St. Pierre never fully recovered. It took until 1970 before the town built its population to one-fifth of what it was before the disaster.

Boer War Is Over

■ British soldiers charge up outcroppings during the Boer War.

The Boer War began in 1899 when the Afrikaner states of the South African Republic attempted to protect their gold-rich land from British **prospectors**. The Afrikaners, or Boers, were descendants of 17th-century Dutch settlers. Many Britons had moved into their territory, and the Boers passed laws to prevent the British from taking control. In response, Britain increased the size of its military in the area. The Boers then ordered the British troops to withdraw or face war. When the British stood fast, the Boers attacked. At first, it seemed an unfair fight. The British had more than 450,000 troops, and the Boers had only about 87,000. Yet the Boers were surprise victors in several battles. After a few British victories, the Boer forces broke into guerrilla groups, attacking British forts and the railroad.

Fighting was intense, and the conflict finally came to an end in 1902. On May 31, 1902, the Treaty of Vereeniging was signed. It made the Boer states part of the British Empire but promised them self-government. Britain agreed to pay millions of dollars to help rebuild the **Transvaal**. The cost of the war was much greater. Afrikaner forces lost about 4,000 soldiers, and more than 20,000 civilians died in concentration camps. Britain lost about 28,000 people in the conflict. Britain also lost its reputation as a formidable military power and ended the Boer War financially drained.

Russia and Japan at War

Japan was unhappy about the Russian occupation of China's eastern province, Manchuria. Japan was also afraid that Russia would capture Korea—a country important to Japan's security. Japan grew increasingly hostile, but Czar Nicholas II of Russia did not want to go to war. Then, in February 1904, Japan attacked Port Arthur, a Russian-controlled city at the tip of the Liaotung Peninsula, west of Korea. This started the Russo-Japanese war. Russia was a strong power, and Japan was virtually unknown in the West. People around the world predicted a quick and bloody end to Japan's attack. They were wrong. Japan proved it was a powerful and skilled opponent. Czar Nicholas reacted slowly to the attacks, not taking the conflict seriously. Even after he realized that Russian forces were losing on all fronts, he would not

back down. His country's pride and honor were at stake. He launched attacks, but could not defeat the Japanese. In the end, Russia and Japan accepted President Roosevelt's offer to **mediate** the conflict. On September 5, 1905, the two sides signed the Treaty of Portsmouth. Russia agreed to pull out of Liaoyang, Manchuria, and Port

■ After more than 5,000 sailors died in the Battle of Tsushima, Russia agreed to peace talks.

Arthur, and it gave Japan the southern half of Sakhalin. It also recognized Japan's influence over Korea. Japan had won the war, but the cost in dollars and lives was high on both sides.

A Cordial Understanding

Traditionally, France and Britain had not seen eye to eye, but they decided to put their differences aside for the good of both countries. In 1904, the leaders signed the Entente Cordiale, which translates as "cordial understanding." The agreement stated that Britain and France would support each other and their **colonial** efforts, especially in northern Africa. This new Anglo-French friendship worried Kaiser Wilhelm II, Emperor of Germany. He attempted to test the entente by declaring himself protector of Moroccan independence—a subject of interest to France. His efforts only made the pact stronger. In 1907, Russia joined the Anglo-French alliance, creating the Triple Entente. The stage was being set for World War I.

The President Is Dead

President William McKinley was attending the Pan-American Exposition in Buffalo, New York, on September 6, 1901. He greeted supporters and then encountered a man with a hankerchief over his right hand. That hankerchief hid a weapon. Two shots exploded from Leon Czolgosz's gun, hitting the president. Agents tackled the assassin, and McKinley's plea that they not hurt the man likely saved him from being beaten to death. The president fought for life for seven days

■ **William McKinley was the governor of Ohio before he became president.**

before dying from his wounds on September 14. He was only six months into his second term in office. Czolgosz, an **anarchist**, was executed the following month in Auburn, New York.

Anarchists across the country were arrested following the shooting. Most of them criticized Czolgosz's actions. People who spoke against the fallen president were fired from their jobs or beaten. The country was in a state of shock over the assassination of its leader. McKinley was the third president to be assassinated in less than fifty years. To make matters worse, White House officials could not locate Vice President Theodore Roosevelt—he was hunting in upstate New York. For twelve hours, the U.S. did not have a leader. Once Roosevelt was reached with the news, he returned to Washington and was sworn in as the twenty-sixth president.

> **"Goodbye, goodbye all...It is God's way. His will, not ours, be done."**
>
> President McKinley on his deathbed

New Territory

In 1898, the U.S. took over the Hawai'ian Islands. On June 14, 1900, Congress officially declared Hawai'i a U.S. territory. All the Hawai'ians living there instantly became U.S. citizens. The U.S. government thought the group of islands could provide a gateway to Asia, and it hoped to increase trade with the Far East. The islands would also be a great location to build military bases. Hawai'i was located about halfway to another U.S. possession, the Philippines.

The territory's first governor was Sanford B. Dole, a former Republican president and plantation owner. The development of canneries made the islands a valuable pineapple provider. While **annexation** was a sound political move, it was hard for Hawai'ians to accept. The arrival of Europeans and Americans had led to the erosion of Hawai'ian religion, land, and independence. Hawai'i did not become a state until 1959.

Keeping It Green

President Theodore Roosevelt was an environmentalist long before there was such a movement. As he traveled the country, he admired the beauty of the land. He wanted to preserve it so that future generations could share his enjoyment. Roosevelt set 150 million acres of public land aside as protected natural areas. Businesses and industry could not develop or exploit the resources here. Roosevelt then added another 85 million acres in Alaska and the Northwest. In 1902, Roosevelt introduced the Reclamation Act. This provided **irrigation** and other important services for western land. The Roosevelt Dam was built near Phoenix, Arizona, to provide water for the arid state.

The president's concern for natural resources and areas prompted him to establish the Congress of Governors in 1908. Representatives from all the states, as well as experts and legislators, came together to discuss national policy in regard to natural resources. While some members of Congress disagreed with the president's spending, the convention was the start of conservation in the U.S.

■ The Roosevelt Dam took nearly eight years to build.

WELCOME OKLAHOMA

■ For years, Oklahoma Territory had been fighting for statehood. Many times, it had nearly become a U.S. state, independent of the Indian Territory around it. In 1906, Congress decided to bring the two areas together into one state. The Indian Territory was no longer a separate political unit, and all the Native Americans living in it were made U.S. citizens. Discussions about Oklahoma began on November 20, 1906. By the summer of 1907, the committee meetings were finished, and in September, territorial votes to approve the constitution were underway. One of the terms of joining was that citizens be allowed to write their own laws and submit them to a direct vote.

Another provision allowed voters to accept or reject laws made by the legislature. The Territory's constitution also stated that all high state officials had to be elected. On November 16, 1907, President Roosevelt welcomed Oklahoma as the forty-sixth state in the Union.

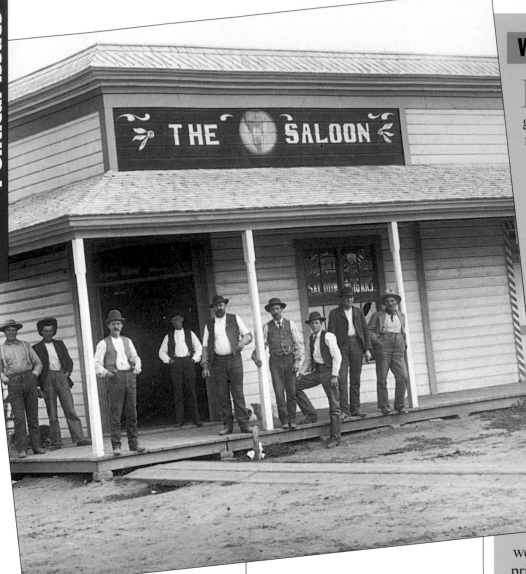

■ Citizens gather on a porch in front of the Globe Saloon in Drewsey, Oregon.

War with Trusts

President Theodore Roosevelt broke new ground and redefined the responsibilities and duties of a U.S. president. In 1902 he prosecuted the Northern Securities Company for **violating** the Sherman Antitrust Act of 1890. This Act said that mergers could not be set up to achieve a monopoly—to get control over a market. The Northern Securities Company was a group of railroad companies that operated as though they were one company. By doing this, they had little competition from other companies and so were able to set their own prices. Such companies were also called trusts. Roosevelt told his attorney general, Philander C. Knox, to sue the company. This sent a clear message to U.S. businesses—the government was going to enforce this law strongly. It also indicated to companies that their interests were second to those of the country. The Northern Securities Company was ordered to dissolve. This action did not start a flood of antitrust actions, but it did establish a **precedent** on which to fall back.

Anti-Saloon Movement

After the Civil War, the population rose and so did the number of saloons. Starting in 1873, thousands of women began marching to saloons demanding that the owners fold their businesses and stop selling alcohol. By 1900, the men and women involved in the anti-saloon movement numbered in the millions. They viewed saloons as the main cause of violence and family breakdowns. The Anti-Saloon League of America (ASL) arose in Ohio and spurred people into political action. State branches of the organization supported candidates for public office. Members insisted that their state governments allow people to vote "yes" or "no" on whether to continue to license saloons. By 1916, twenty-three of the forty-eight states had passed anti-saloon laws. This closed down saloons and stopped the manufacturing of alcohol. By 1919, the ASL's efforts were realized with the passing of the eighteenth amendment of the constitution—**prohibition**.

Taking the Office

While fighting the Spanish-American War, Theodore Roosevelt had complained about the beef his soldiers were given. He said he would sooner have eaten his hat. Preparation of meat and other food had never been regulated. Roosevelt released a report that criticized how meat was processed. He was not alone in his concerns. In his novel *The Jungle*, Upton Sinclair told about disturbing conditions in America's meat-packing plants. By 1906, Congress had passed a law that allowed meat inspections at packing plants. It led to the Pure Food and Drug Act, which ensured that food and medicines were safe.

Roosevelt also addressed concerns about railroads. Unfair fees and unsafe practices were on the top of the list of issues. Roosevelt pushed for some government regulation of the railroads but left ownership in private hands. The 1906 Hepburn Act allowed the Interstate Commerce Commission to set maximum rates and to enforce these limits. Railroads were given thirty days to obey the decision.

■ Theodore Roosevelt is considered to be one of the most successful presidents in U.S. history.

BY POPULAR VOTE

■ Theodore Roosevelt wanted to win the presidency on his own merits. The charismatic politician got his wish. In 1904, Roosevelt won the Republican nomination handily. The Democrats were disappointed with how their candidate, William Jennings Bryan, had done in 1900. They chose Alton B. Parker, a conservative judge from New York, as his replacement. Parker was no match for President Roosevelt. Minority groups, military veterans, and many reformers looked to Roosevelt to continue leading the country. He won by a landslide—drawing 336 electoral votes to Parker's 140. It was the largest margin of victory in three decades. Roosevelt took the presidency, with Charles W. Fairbanks as second in command.

> "I am no longer a political accident."
>
> Theodore Roosevelt, after the election

A "Nobel" Man

In 1906, President Roosevelt became the first American to win the prestigious Nobel Peace Prize. He was recognized for his involvement in bringing the Russo-Japanese war to an end. The U.S. was friendly toward both warring countries. As a result, Roosevelt acted as a mediator between the two sides. In the spring of 1905, he began working on a solution. By August, he had convinced Russia and Japan to send diplomats to the U.S. to discuss a possible peace agreement. The president then helped negotiate the terms of the peace solution. The Treaty of Portsmouth, which came out of the peace conference held in Portsmouth, New Hampshire, was signed in September 1905. Its passage signaled the official end to the conflict.

The Jungle Message

Upton Sinclair was more than a writer. He was also a social and economic reformer. He ran for the Socialist Party but was not elected. This did not affect his dedication to social and economic issues, though. He used his books to get his message out. His 1906 novel caused a great deal of controversy. It even caught the attention of the president. *The Jungle* described, in vivid detail, the unsanitary manner in which meat was processed and handled in Chicago's stockyards. It also exposed the terrible working conditions at packing plants. Sinclair's novel sparked President Roosevelt to pass laws for government inspections of meat packers. *The Jungle* magnified Sinclair's reputation, and he used his fame to open Americans' eyes to other abuses. His political and social novels looked at many

■ Upton Sinclair wrote 90 books in his career, including his autobiography in 1962.

industries, including the media. Not all of Sinclair's books were critical. His eleven-book series of adventure stories about Lanny Budd, a U.S. secret agent, was very popular. Sinclair won the 1943 Pulitzer Prize in fiction for his novel *Dragon's Teeth* (1942).

Master of Fiction

Henry James contrasted the conservative innocence of America and the more liberal European cultures. His early novels often explored the impact of European life on Americans living in or visiting Europe. These books include *Daisy Miller* (1879) and *The Portrait of a Lady* (1881). James, who was living in London, began writing about the English way of life in such novels as *The Tragic Muse* (1890) and *The Awkward Age* (1899). James soon returned to the clash of U.S. and European cultures with *The Wings of the Dove* (1902), *The Ambassadors* (1903), and *The Golden Bowl* (1904).

James wrote complex works that were driven by strong characters rather than by dramatic events or complicated stories. Important details about the characters and the plot were introduced through conversations between characters and through one character's observations about another. James's novels and essays were successful, and his profound influence on literature in both Europe and America was finally appreciated in the 1940s.

OFF TO SEE THE WIZARD

■ L. Frank Baum worked in the newspaper industry from 1880 to 1902. Baum's hometown of Chittenango, New York, is a long way from Kansas, the starting point of his most famous novel. With *The Wonderful Wizard of Oz*, which was published in 1900, Baum created an all-new children's fairyland. Incredible creatures and adventures awaited any reader who explored the land of Oz. In it, the central character, Dorothy, falls asleep in Kansas during a tornado and wakes up in Oz. Readers share Dorothy's journey to see the Wizard, the only one who can help her get home. On the way, she meets a scarecrow, a tin man, and a lion, who each want to see the Wizard as well.

The book was such a success that in 1901, Baum created a musical out of the stories—*The Wizard of Oz*. Before his death in 1919, he penned thirteen additional books about Oz. After he died, many others carried on the series. Actress Judy Garland and her little dog, Toto, brought the story to the big screen in 1939. The story and the film became children's classics.

London Answers the Call of the Wild

Jack London's 1903 novel, *The Call of the Wild*, has everything an adventure story needs. Set during the gold rush of 1897, it is the story of a sled dog named Buck. After his owner dies, the dog runs into the wild and ends up leading a wolf pack. The book was an instant success. Many of London's novels appealed to people's romantic sense of the outdoors. For story material, he drew on his varied experiences and jobs, ranging from waterfront pirate and Alaskan gold miner to socialist speaker. With *The Call of the Wild,* London was trying to present something significant. This novel showed civilization's often scary attraction to the wild world, and readers around the globe could relate to its message. The novel was translated into fifty languages and made London a celebrity. His success did not change his routine— London continued to write for fifteen hours each day. Some of

his other works include *People of the Abyss* (1903), *The Sea Wolf* (1904), *White Fang* (1906), and *Martin Eden* (1909). In his career, London wrote approximately 200 short stories,

■ Jack London often said that he wrote to pay for his Beauty Ranch in Glen Ellen, California.

400 articles, and about 50 books of fiction and nonfiction.

Army Experiments

Dr. James Carroll became very ill on August 27, 1900. So did his colleague Dr. Jess William Lazear. The two were part of a team headed by Major Walter Reed sent by the U.S. army to study mosquitoes in Cuba. They set out to prove that yellow fever was the result of mosquito bites. Volunteers from the ranks stepped forward to take part in the experiments. Private John R. Kissinger and others like him refused to accept the $250 payment for the experiments—they felt it was their duty, and they were acting in the interests of humankind. Kissinger was paralyzed, Carroll recovered with heart damage, and Lazear died. Their sacrifices saved the lives of millions. Through the experiments, Reed proved that the mosquito species *Stegomyia fasciata* carried the disease. These insects picked up yellow fever from victims by drawing blood in the first three days of the individual's sickness. Then it took another twelve days for their bite to become potent. Yellow fever can lead to delirium, coma, or even death.

Model T

Although thousands of Oldsmobiles were motoring along U.S. streets by 1902, these were luxury cars, and most people could not afford them. Then, in 1903, automobile engineer Henry Ford took a chance. He formed the Ford Motor Company. Ford did not want his automobiles to just be toys for the rich, so he began to make his own parts rather than simply assembling parts from other companies. This cut his costs and allowed him to make less expensive cars. By 1906, Ford's cars were being made from steel, making them stronger, lighter, and faster than any other. For a year, Ford and his team worked on a new design. The result was the Model T, introduced in October 1908. For $850, Americans could buy a sturdy vehicle that stood up to potholes. Ford sold 18,664 cars from 1909 to 1910. The number nearly doubled the following year. In the 1910s, Ford refined his methods, creating the automobile assembly line. This meant he could offer cars for even less money.

■ In the 1900s, the 20-horsepower, 4-cylinder Model T was the most affordable car on the market.

Flying High

Orville and Wilbur Wright's bicycle shop developed into something else altogether—an air travel laboratory. The Wrights decided that they would design an airplane and learn to fly it. Over the next few years, the brothers studied airborne objects. In 1900, they built a kite that could support a pilot. They tested their inventions and continued to try out new models. On December 17, 1903, the Wright brothers thought they had eliminated all potential problems. They were right. The Wright biplane took flight at Kill Devil Hills near Kitty Hawk, North Carolina. This new design had a wingspan of 39 feet and weighed 750 pounds, pilot included. Orville made the first successful flight, staying in the air for twelve seconds.

■ Orville's first flight in 1903 covered a distance of 120 feet.

In 1904, the Wrights added a 16-horsepower engine to their plane. They were able to fly farther and execute tighter turns in this machine. By 1905, the brothers been contracted to design airplanes for the U.S. War Department. In the following years, they patented their invention and looked for buyers. In 1908, they gave the first public showing of the planes in the U.S. Orville set a record by keeping the plane in the air for more than an hour on September 9. They then showed their planes in Europe, and many countries took notice. With orders flowing in, the brothers established the airplane-manufacturing Wright Company.

Bigger Is Best

The world's first electric underground railway was built in London, England, in 1890. It was a celebrated feat, but New York City topped it. It built the world's biggest subway in October 1904. This system of transportation was a necessity. Above-ground traffic had become too crowded and would only get worse as the population grew. The public rail system was a popular solution to the problem. The train ran from the Brooklyn Bridge uptown to Broadway at 145th Street. On its first day, about 500,000 people stepped aboard to experience the underground system for themselves. The cars sped along the 15 miles of track at 25 miles per hour. As promised, the subway system took New Yorkers from Harlem to City Hall in fifteen minutes. It was not a complete success, though. The mass of people created an opportunity for crime. On the very first day, at 7:00 in the evening, a thief stole a $500 diamond pin from a subway passenger. Despite the risks, the subway was a welcome escape from the heavy traffic on the streets of New York.

Fighting for the Title

Jack Johnson was not intimidated by Tommy Burns, the world heavyweight boxing champion. Instead, he set out to take his title. For two years, Johnson challenged Burns to a bout. Even though Burns thought he might lose, he needed the money, so he agreed to fight. In 1908, the title match between Johnson and Burns finally arrived. Johnson fought hard. His strength and raw ability overpowered Burns, the smallest heavyweight champion ever. The police stepped

in to stop the intense beating. Johnson claimed the title after a battle that had lasted fourteen rounds. With the decision, Johnson became the first African American to win the heavyweight crown. Some people disputed the win, but Johnson went on to defend his title until 1915, when he lost to American Jess Willard in the twenty-sixth round.

■ Jack Johnson boxed professionally for twenty-seven years.

Heroic on the Mound

Denton True Young had a fearsome fastball. It earned him the nickname Cyclone—Cy for short. Young was the best pitcher baseball ever knew. He began his career in Cleveland when he was 23 years old. In his first game, Young allowed only three batters to hit and led his team to an 8-1 victory. His performance only improved from there. Young left Cleveland for the St. Louis Cardinals in 1898 and then joined the Boston Red Sox in 1901. In 1903, Boston was fighting for the World Series title. In game five, the team

> "I thought I had to show all my stuff and I almost tore the boards off the grandstand with my fastball."
>
> Cy Young on his appearance in the first World Series

put its hopes on Young. He did not let them down. He allowed only six batters to hit, and he hit three of his own for good measure. The Sox won the game 11-2. In his three starts during that series, Young won two of them and helped his team to victory in the first World Series championship. At 36 years of age, Young was just getting warmed up.

On May 5, 1906, Young became the first pitcher in the

Major Leagues to pitch a perfect game—no opposition player reached first base. He boasted no-hitters three times in his twenty-two-year career. During the 1900s, Young averaged twenty-seven wins per year and an impressive earned-run average of only 2.12. Young's name appears many times in the record books. He holds the league record for complete games (751), career wins (511), and innings pitched (7,356). He retired in 1911 and was inducted into the Baseball Hall of Fame in 1937. Each year, the Cy Young Award is given to the best big-league pitcher.

Olympic Triumphs

The 1900 Olympic Games were held in Paris, France. More than 1,200 athletes arrived from 26 countries to compete for the silver and bronze medals—there was no gold medal during the decade. University of Pennsylvania roommates Alvin Kraenzlein, Irving Baxter, and John Tewksbury were joined by Lafayette, Indiana, native Ray Ewry to form an incredible track-and-field team. They controlled the twenty-three track-and-field events, winning eleven, finishing second in five, and third in one. Kraenzlein is the only track athlete to win four individual titles in one year. Baxter led the medals with two first-place finishes and three second-place finishes. U.S. athletes also took home medals in other events. The polo team shared a victory with Great Britain, and the tug-of-war team claimed second place. In golf, Charles Sands won the men's singles event. The coxed eights rowing team also won their event. The 1900 games were the first to allow women to compete. American Marion Jones finished third in women's singles tennis, and Margaret Abbott won the women's singles golf title, with Daria Pratt placing third.

Football Fatalities

Americans were shocked by the increasing number of serious injuries and even deaths that occurred on the football field. Before 1906, teams relied on brute strength and outweighing the opposition to win games. In 1904 alone, there were 18 deaths and 159 injuries during college football games. College representatives knew they had to take action to protect their players. Several colleges had banned or threatened to ban football. Then, in 1906, the Intercollegiate Athletic Association made a number of rule changes to try to make the game safer. One of these changes was to allow the forward pass. The association also created a new neutral zone. This area lay between the offensive and defensive lines. Also, the offense now had to have at least six players on the line of scrimmage before the play was started. Representatives hoped that this would help protect players and achieve safety in the sport.

■ In the 1900s, few players wore helmets. Football helmets were not mandatory until the 1930s.

Dribbling Dynamos

In 1891, Dr. James Naismith invented basketball in Springfield, Massachusetts. It did not take long for basketball to become a popular sport. In 1901, several post-secondary schools joined to create the New England Intercollegiate Basketball League. Using a soccer ball, players had to move the ball down the court by batting it from hand to hand. Then they shot the soccer ball into one of the two peach baskets, which were closed at the bottom and hung at either end of the court. By 1906, a metal rim with a net hanging below it replaced the peach baskets. The net was cut to allow the ball to drop through. Soon, a ball made especially for the sport was introduced. It was built from leather panels sewn together with a rubber balloon inside. This balloon of air gave the ball its bounce. Players could

now run down the court while bouncing, or dribbling, the ball. The rules stated that once the players stopped dribbling, they had to pass the ball. In 1916, a change in the rules allowed players to shoot after dribbling. The rules around fouls changed as well. At the beginning, a player who received two personal fouls had to sit out

James Naismith (center) was inducted into the Basketball Hall of Fame in 1959.

until the next shot was made. In 1908, players were allowed five fouls per game. Once they had received five, they had to sit out for the rest of the game. This same year, glass backboards were introduced.

Passing the Puck

The game of ice hockey was created in the mid-1800s in Canada. By the 1890s, amateur leagues and teams had spread through Canada and the northern U.S. Many U.S. colleges in the region had school hockey clubs. Players slowly began molding the game into the sport we know today. Padding was developed for protection, and arenas were built to house the sport. Before 1902, it was seen as "ungentlemanly"

to accept payment for playing on a team. Most players played simply for the love of the game. After 1902, leagues began to pay their players openly. In 1904, the first professional hockey league was formed in Houghton, Michigan. The league had teams stationed in Calumet, Houghton, and Sault Ste. Marie, Michigan, as well as in Pittsburgh, Pennsylvania. There was also a team from Sault Ste. Marie, Ontario, in Canada, so the league's name was changed

to the International Pro Hockey League. Many similar leagues followed this one, including the National Hockey Association in 1909 and the Pacific Coast Hockey Association in 1911. The two leagues were fiercely competitive and often found themselves fighting over money and players. In 1917, the Pacific Coast Hockey Association merged with the Western Canada Hockey League to create the National Hockey League (NHL).

Queen of the Courts

May Sutton was born in England in 1886 but grew up in Pasadena, California. It was there that she learned to play tennis. She was dedicated to being the best player possible. At 12 years old, Sutton played in her first tournament, and by the following year, she had won the first of her many Pacific Southwest championships.

In 1904, Sutton shocked the tennis world when she claimed the U.S. title. She was the youngest women's champion in history. That record was unbeaten for eighty years until Tracy Austin won the tournament at the age of sixteen years, nine months. With the U.S. title under her belt, Sutton worked toward England's Wimbledon championship. Marion Jones was the first U.S. player to enter that competition. She competed at the prestigious tournament in 1900 but lost in the quarterfinals. Sutton wanted not only to enter but to win the championship. In 1905, she did just that. Thanks to her determination, Sutton was crowned the women's singles champion. She attracted attention for other reasons, too. Her short skirts, which exposed her ankles, and her vest-cut shirtsleeves, which showed off her arms, caused a stir. Despite the controversy, Sutton repeated her victory at Wimbledon in 1907.

■ May Sutton's powerful forehand helped her make tennis history.

Marathon Disgrace

The marathon lost some of its luster at the 1904 Olympic Games in St. Louis, Missouri. One runner was chased a mile off course by a dog, and the hot weather prevented seventeen of the other thirty-one racers from finishing. In the end, American Fred Lorz was the first to cross the finish line. The crowd went wild, but officials soon discovered that Lorz had not finished at all. At the 9-mile point, he had suffered from cramps and dropped out of the race. An official drove him to the stadium to get his street clothes. Lorz decided to run in and break the winner's tape as a joke. He carried the gag too far by accepting the winning medal. Lorz was banned from competition but was reinstated the next year. The true winner of the marathon was American Thomas Hicks. He finished the race in three hours, twenty-eight minutes, fifty-three seconds. That is the worst marathon time in Olympic history. Hicks was helped over the finish line. In a final twist to the marathon, Cuban Felix Carvajal, competing in his street clothes, paused at an apple orchard for a snack. He became sick from the rotten fruit and had to rest. He eventually got up and stumbled to the finish line. He still came in fourth.

Carry Nation Means Business

Carry Nation was serious about prohibition. She tried to protest peacefully against people who operated saloons and sold alcohol by lecturing and holding public prayers. When these seemed to have little effect, she tried a new tactic. With a hatchet in hand, Nation and her "Home Defenders' Army" smashed saloons

> "Oh, I tell you, ladies, you never know what joy it gives you to start out to smash a rumshop."
>
> Carry Nation, in her lectures to women

throughout Kansas. This army of several hundred, led by the grandmotherly Nation, insisted that the government make people obey the laws against producing and drinking alcohol. Not everyone appreciated her efforts. She was arrested thirty times for disturbing the peace. She paid for bail and fines with the money she earned from her lectures and from selling souvenir hatchets. Nation's crusade carried her across the country, smashing the illegal saloons in hundreds of towns.

An Inspirational Woman

Helen Keller would not let anything get in her way, least of all the physical challenges she faced. Many people thought nothing could be done to educate the young Keller. At 19 months old, she had suffered an illness that left her both deaf and blind. No one knew how to communicate with her until she was seven. Anne Mansfield Sullivan from the Perkins Institute for the Blind taught Keller to read Braille and write using a special typewriter. She also developed a system of spelling out words on Keller's hand to communicate. In 1890, Keller learned to speak. She was a quick student, and she surprised many people when she entered Radcliffe College. She graduated with honors in 1904. Keller devoted the rest of her life to social causes.

Keller served on the Massachusetts Commission

■ Helen Keller, Anne Sullivan, and Alexander Graham Bell come together for a historic meeting.

for the Blind and helped raise funds for the American Foundation for the Blind. She lectured around the world about physical disabilities, reaching audiences as distant as Europe and South Africa. Keller was an **advocate** of women's **suffrage**, socialism, and the abilities of those with physical challenges. She wrote several books,

including *The Story of My Life* (1902), *The World I Live In* (1908), and *Teacher: Anne Sullivan Macy* (1955). Through Keller's success, Americans realized the power of the human spirit and will.

Made to Order

Shopping was made easier in the 1900s. Americans could buy almost anything they needed through mail-order houses. Montgomery Ward led the charge with its slogan "Supplier for Every Trade and Calling on Earth." The enormous department store created a catalog from which Americans could order a wide range of goods, including toys, tools, and clothes. It was the first mail-order catalog in the world. To become better known, Montgomery Ward sent out more than 3 million copies free of charge in 1904. The 4-pound book usually cost fifteen cents. Americans scrambled to order their fashions and farm equipment through the mail. Ward guaranteed to give people their money back if they wanted to return the goods they had ordered. This gave people confidence. No longer did they have to rely on local stores. Regardless of where they lived, they could spend a pleasant evening poring over the catalog's many treasures.

Pushing for Change

In 1905, a group of twenty-nine prominent African Americans met to discuss political rights and **segregation**. Included in this group was sociologist and activist W. E. B. Du Bois. Hotels on the U.S. side of Niagara Falls would not give them rooms, so the meeting was held on the Canadian side of the Falls. The group released a **manifesto** that demanded full civil, economic, and political rights for all Americans. The committee decided to hold their movement's anniversary on Abraham Lincoln's birthday. February 12 marked the beginning of the organization's efforts to improve the living conditions of African Americans in the U.S. Sixty people gathered in New York in 1909 to try to put an end to the worsening violence and mistreatment of African Americans. The push came after a riot in Springfield, Illinois, where some residents had attempted to force African-American citizens out of town.

The civil rights group became the National Association for the Advancement of Colored People (NAACP) in 1910. Du Bois was one of its founding members.

■ W. E. B Du Bois is considered to be one of the greatest scholars of his time.

Union Protection

Before 1900, most women workers in the clothing industry were without legal protection. They often worked seventy hours per week for thirty cents a day. In June 1900, eleven delegates from seven local New York unions came together to create the International Ladies' Garment Workers Union (ILGWU) in order to protect the workers. There were already about 2,000 garment workers represented by the local unions. Most women who initially joined the union were Jewish immigrants working in **sweatshops**. The strength of the union quickly grew. In 1909, the ILGWU fought against the terrible working conditions with a strike in New York City. Thousands of people walked off the job. This action became known as the "Uprising of the 20,000." Another strike in 1910 helped bring about change—the women were given higher wages and overtime pay, as well as safer and more comfortable working conditions. It was the first major settlement between garment companies and the ILGWU. The strikes brought people's attention to the problems and also to the existence and strength of the union.

Billion-Dollar Business

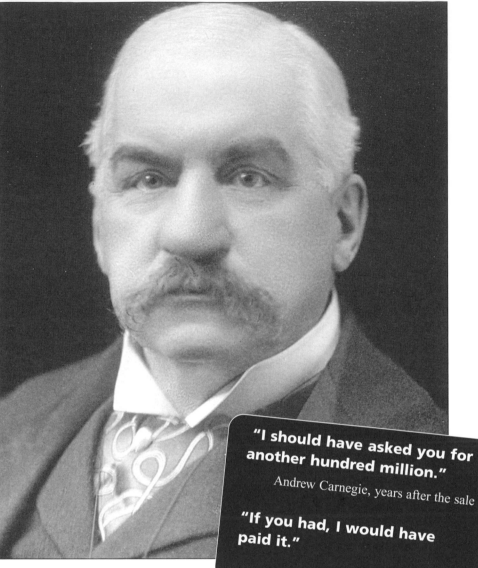

"I should have asked you for another hundred million."

Andrew Carnegie, years after the sale

"If you had, I would have paid it."

J. P. Morgan

■ J. P. Morgan was the nation's wealthiest man at the turn of the century.

In 1901, the sale of the Carnegie Steel Corporation to J. P. Morgan for $492 million made Andrew Carnegie the wealthiest man in the world. The company controlled about one-quarter of the steel and iron production in the U.S. Carnegie retired from business and focused his attention and his fortunes on charity work. Morgan, on the other hand, built on Carnegie's success with the corporation and turned it into U.S. Steel, the first billion-dollar company. To do this, Morgan bought many other large metal companies. U.S. Steel dominated mines, mills, and factories, producing more than 8 billion tons of steel every year. U.S. Steel produced more steel than most countries in the world. In the first year of its sale, U.S. Steel earned $90 million, and it continued to prosper throughout the decade. Looking back, Carnegie realized what a bargain J. P. Morgan had received.

Money Panic

On October 22, 1907, rumors that the banks could collapse caused a rush of people to withdraw their savings. By the end of the day, the Knickerbocker Bank in New York City was out of money. Other banks experienced the same panic, and within a few days, it had spread across the country.

The Department of Commerce and Labor, which was established in 1903, was in charge of the nation's economic interests. At the time, banks depended on their own monetary resources. Their stability could be affected by financial difficulties or even rumors. That is what happened in New York City. A drop in copper prices started a crisis. The market for copper mining stocks fell, causing banks with heavy interest in copper to **fluctuate**.

President Roosevelt took action. He sent his secretary of the treasury, George B. Cortelyou, to work with financiers, including J. P. Morgan, to help stabilize the banks. Private bankers also pledged $100 million in gold to save the banks. The government promised that the banks were secure. To make sure of it, Roosevelt placed money in some New York banks that were in trouble. That seemed to ease the panic, but the government did not look into why the panic had happened, nor did it reimburse lost money or put a system in place to prevent another panic in the future. It took until 1913 for the government to improve the banking and monetary systems with the introduction of the Federal Reserve System.

Stock Scares

In 1901, the New York Stock Exchange suffered a significant loss. Prices fell drastically as stockholders sold, sold, sold. Large railroads bore the brunt of the fall. The Reading, Great Northern, Northern Pacific, and Union Pacific rail lines dropped ten to eleven points. Analysts blamed the crash on banks that needed short-term money and therefore sold stocks. Despite the losses, trading remained steady at 2.2 million shares. The market never reached the level of panic that it experienced in 1907, however, when a rush of selling caused stock prices to plummet. The market suffered the worst single-day drop since 1901. To make matters worse, the 1907 crash came after a long period of falling prices, which businesses blamed on President

Roosevelt's attempt to break up trusts. The stock plunge led to a **recession** in the U.S. that lasted until 1909.

■ Established in 1792, the New York Stock Exchange is one of the largest trading markets in the world.

Hairy Situation

There was now a solution for women with hopelessly straight hair. Permanents, or perms, were first introduced in 1906. This was not an everyday hairstyle.

To achieve permanent waves, women had to pay dearly. The technique cost $1,000 and took eight to twelve hours to complete. Women who could not spend so much money on a hairstyle turned to the pompadour. Hair was combed high off the forehead and then piled on top of the head. This style, also called Gibson Girl hair and the psyche knot, was very popular. French twists and smaller, more controlled styles were often worn, too.

Men followed fashion trends as well. By the beginning of the century, many men traded their large mustaches and beards for clean shaves. However, a wide variety of styles were available for men of the 1900s. Some men preferred well-groomed mustaches and small beards. Facial hair was controlled and styled using wax. Sideburns continued to be popular, but they were shorter than in previous decades. Some men chose to wear muttonchops and chin beards trimmed to a point. Still others kept the longer, bushier mustaches.

Unnatural Posture

"The effect [of the corset] was as if the top of the lady was a foot ahead of the rest of her."
Author Elizabeth Ewing

■ Women would be tightly laced into their corsets to achieve the "perfect" shape.

"The health corset" hit the market in 1900. Along with some extra fabric at the back, this corset gave women's bodies an S-shape, something like that of a kangaroo. Dressing in the 1900s was a complicated business. Women wore many layers of clothing every day, regardless of the temperature. They first put on underlayers of the dress, belts, drawers, linings for the skirt, and a rigid layer or boning to give dresses their shape. Then came the petticoats, which added volume to the dress—the dress fabric was never near the woman's legs. Extra fabric, called a bustle, was added to women's backsides to achieve the "S" effect. Their upper bodies were hidden under corsets and vests. These vests created the top arc of the "S," and the fabric, petticoats, liners, and boning created the bottom arc. Many women were relieved to see this style loosen up in 1907.

At the beginning of the century, women's fashions followed the trends of the previous decade. Fashionable women wore tightly fitted corsets under layers of decorative fabric. One purpose of a woman's wardrobe was to show her father's or husband's wealth and status. As a result, it was only wealthy women who had the time and money to follow the latest trends and own the most stylish hats and petticoats. Middle-class women copied the fashions they saw in magazines and newspapers. They showed styles to dressmakers to reproduce, or sewed their own versions of the day's look.

As the decade progressed, fashion began to change. The fresh ideas of Parisian designer Paul Poiret brought a new look to American women. The S-shape gave way to Poiret's straight, high-waisted classical styles. By 1908, the Straight Line allowed dresses to fall around the body in a narrow column. Designs were more natural—and more comfortable. Still, Poiret's designs had their faults. His clothes required a different type of corset that reached the knees. Standing was easy, but sitting down posed some challenges. Later, Poiret designed the narrow hobble skirt, which made walking difficult.

The Price of Fashion

In 1900, women's styles became less ornamented. Designers experimented with two-piece outfits that had high necks and tight sleeves. Bustles were abandoned for smoother lines. This simplicity did not translate into comfort. American women were expected to fit a specific mold. Those who did not fit it tried to squeeze their bodies into shape by using corsets. Paris fashion designers stated that 18 inches was the perfect waist measurement. Women around the world fainted while trying to cinch themselves into corsets to fit this standard. Dresses were tight to the hip and flared wide at the bottom to hide a woman's real shape. Respectable women did not show any skin on their arms or neck, so many women were covered in fabric, even in the heat of summer. Women who played sports had to

In the 1900s, bathing suits were often woolen dresses worn with gloves, hats, and woolen stockings.

do so in skirts that reached their ankles. Even bathing suits, which were seen as short and revealing, reached the mid-calf. Women were not the only ones to cover up. Now that mixed-gender public swimming was popular, men had to cover their chests. Men's swimsuits were made up of a tank shirt and shorts.

Fire Makes Immigrants Residents

The 1906 San Francisco earthquake was a disaster for most residents, but for some, it had a positive outcome. The fires had destroyed all of the immigration records in the city. Because of this, many immigrants who were in the city at the time were given new citizenship documents. Most of the immigrants had already gone through the proper immigration procedures, but some were able to gain citizenship by simply being in the right place at the right time. Their "paper" citizenship meant that they had "paper" children in other countries who were also eligible to come to the U.S. Still, immigration officials examined each claim carefully to be certain that the "paper citizens" had, in fact, entered the country legally.

Asian Restrictions

In the early 1900s, some parts of U.S. society became alarmed at the growing number of Asian immigrants in the cities. In 1905, the Asiatic Exclusion League was formed to attempt to try and halt the Japanese "invasion." That year, the San Francisco school board began to teach Japanese students separately. This segregation worried President Roosevelt. He said he would restrict Japanese immigration if the city would take back the rule about Japanese students. This gave rise to the Gentleman's Agreement of 1908. The Japanese government agreed to no longer give out labor visas to those who wanted to work in the U.S. Despite these restrictions, many states continued to pass laws against the Japanese.

Korean immigrants were also targeted. The Korean population was much smaller than that of the Japanese. During the 1900s, some Korean students had come to the U.S. to study. There were also some political refugees, but most of the Koreans had

■ Restrictive laws made it difficult for Asians to immigrate to the U.S. in the early 1900s.

originally been laborers on Hawai'ian plantations who moved to the West Coast of the U.S. The increased number of Asian immigrants caused a stir. They were as unwelcome as the Japanese. Korean immigration was soon restricted. Japan, which controlled Korea, eagerly agreed to stop Koreans from entering the U.S. It did not want them competing with Japanese immigrants for work. Regardless of their country of origin, most immigrants found life in the U.S. to be challenging but rewarding.

Steady Flow of Newcomers

The steady flow of immigrants at Ellis Island, the headquarters of the U.S. Immigration and Naturalization Services, caused the country's population to skyrocket in 1900. Approximately 100 newcomers were processed every hour, resulting in a population jump of more than 13 million during the decade. The facility at Ellis Island was upgraded to handle 8,000 immigration applicants each day. This worried some Americans because many of the immigrants were from Eastern Europe, unlike most earlier immigrants. People began arguing that these newcomers were largely unskilled and uneducated. They claimed that the immigrants could not contribute to the country's economy or its political system. Life was difficult for immigrants in the 1900s, and many ethnic groups formed tight communities within U.S. cities for support.

■ More than 1 million people passed through Ellis Island in 1907.

BECOMING AMERICAN

■ People from all over the world left their home countries in search of a new life. This search brought many people to the U.S. The chart below shows the number of people who arrived from selected areas of the world between 1901 and 1910:

Country of Origin	Number of Immigrants
Italy	2,045,877
Russia	1,597,306
Hungary	808,511
Austria	668,209
United Kingdom	525,950
Germany	341,498

The "Right" Immigrants

Despite the growing feelings against foreign-born people coming to the U.S., President Roosevelt announced that he was not worried about the large numbers of immigrants. He was angry with Americans who were hostile toward all immigrants. In his yearly address, he stated, "There is no danger in having too many immigrants of the right kind." The "right kind" of immigrant was one who was willing to learn English and adopt U.S. customs and values. Roosevelt felt that such people would improve themselves through education and would work hard. The "right" immigrant would have respect for and obey the laws. Most of the newcomers to the U.S., especially younger immigrants, wanted to become part of U.S. society, and were eager to be "right." President Roosevelt's dream of a **melting pot** society was carried on by many later presidents.

King of Ragtime

■ Scott Joplin wrote more than 500 pieces of music.

Ragtime would be nothing without Scott Joplin. This composer and pianist was one of the major developers of this upbeat style of music. He taught himself to play the piano and learned classical music from a neighbor. He began working as a musician in Texarkana, Texas, before moving to Missouri. In 1899, he earned a name for himself by publishing "Original Rags" and "Maple Leaf Rag." His many compositions included "Peacherine Rag" (1901), "The Entertainer" (1902), "Palm Leaf Rag—A Slow Drag" (1903), and "Euphoric Sounds" (1909), but they brought only limited attention to ragtime. To help others enjoy music, Joplin opened a teaching studio. By 1907, he was in New York City. There, he published *Treemonisha*, a ragtime piece that he hoped would stand as a unique African-American opera. When it flopped, Joplin was crushed. Long after Joplin's death in 1917, his music enjoyed a revival. The 1973 movie *The Sting* featured Joplin's "The Entertainer" and renewed interest in ragtime.

COMING HOME

■ Of all the songs of the early century, "Bill Bailey, Won't You Please Come Home?" (1902) has stood the test of time. This ragtime piece, written by Hughie Cannon and arranged by Dick Wellstood, had a melody that made people want to sing along to the bouncy tune. The song told the story of a woman who marries a railway man but is still in love with Bill Bailey. Bill Bailey is gone—where, Cannon never says. The song's character is miserable in her relationship and, through her tears, asks for Bailey's return. The song was an enormous smash throughout the country. It was so popular that three spinoff songs were later released, including "When Old Bill Bailey Plays the Ukelele" and "I Wonder Why Bill Bailey Won't Come Home."

American Entertainment

George M. Cohan brought something to Broadway that had been missing—American flair. Most composers were using European styles as the basis for their songs. Cohan looked in his own backyard for inspiration. The result was *Little Johnny Jones* in 1904. This Broadway show had the kind of energy and personality that got toes tapping. With songs such as "Give My Regards to Broadway" and "The Yankee Doodle Boy," this musical stood out. Cohan himself starred as the Yankee Doodle Boy in this show, a role that people associated with him throughout his career. Other Cohan productions included *Forty-five Minutes from Broadway* (1905) and *Seven Keys to Baldpate* (1913). He wrote about twenty plays and musical comedies, in addition to books, lyrics, and music.

Cohan starred in many of his own shows.

George M. Cohan created an entertainment trend with his style of musicals.

Photo By Mi...

SONGS OF THE DAY

Thomas Edison invented the phonograph machine in 1877. He had meant it to be a **dictation** machine for office use. In 1888, German inventor Emile Berliner created the phonograph record. After that, musicians could record songs onto disks that played on the phonograph machine. While not all families had phonograph machines, many Americans enjoyed listening to songs of the decades. Below are some of the songs they listened to:

1900	"A Bird in a Gilded Cage"
1901	"I Love You Truly"
1902	"Bill Bailey, Won't You Please Come Home?"
1902	"In the Good Old Summertime"
1903	"Sweet Adeline"
1904	"When My Golden Hair Has Turned to Silver Gray"
1904	"Meet Me in St. Louis, Louis"
1905	"Wait 'Til the Sun Shines, Nellie"
1906	"Somewhere"
1908	"Take Me Out to the Ball Game"
1908	"It's a Long Way to Tipperary"
1909	"Just a Girl Like You"
1909	"By the Light of the Silvery Moon"

Construction of the Panama Canal began in 1904. The total cost to build it was $350 million.

Taking Panama

In 1901, Britain and the U.S. negotiated the Hay-Poncefote Treaty. This agreement was arranged in order to build and manage a canal across the **isthmus** of Panama. The U.S. Senate would not pass the treaty unless it said that the U.S. could do whatever it needed to defend the canal zone. It also wanted to delete a clause about the involvement of other nations in the area's neutrality. Britain objected to these changes, and another draft was created and submitted to the Senate. This one passed. It stated that the U.S. had control of building and managing the canal. The U.S. also was to be responsible for guaranteeing neutrality, which included building fortifications. The canal was to be available to all nations equally, but the U.S. could restrict its use in times of war. In 1911, Britain said that the U.S. had maneuvered around the last point by passing the Panama Canal Act. This **exempted** Americans from paying canal tolls. President Wilson agreed and repealed the act in 1914.

Philippine Takeover

After the Spanish-American War, the Philippines became the property of the U.S. Filipino revolutionaries were enraged. They refused to recognize U.S. control and fought hard for independence for three long years. The country put its faith in a **provisional** Filipino government in 1898. In February 1899, a Filipino patrol was met with U.S. gunfire. U.S. troops drove the government forces back, and in November, Filipino guerrilla groups took up the fight. Fighting lessened in 1901 with the arrest of rebel leader Emilio Aquinaldo. He pledged allegiance to the U.S., but the conflict continued for another year. The battle ended in 1902, with U.S. forces in control of the archipelago of 7,100 islands. Led by General Arthur MacArthur, the Philippine War was America's first guerrilla conflict in Southeast Asia. The conflict devastated the Philippines. Estimates of casualties range from 50,000 to 2 million. Many people criticized the U.S. for what they saw as a slaughter.

Cuban Territory

American troops had occupied Cuba since the end of the Spanish-American War in 1898. The countries agreed that the U.S. would control Cuba, and by 1899, American troops had taken over. The U.S. kept its promise to allow Cuba to govern itself, but only by those leaders who followed democratic rules and were "Americanized." Despite American efforts to control the government, Cuban separatists won a majority of the seats in the assembly in 1900. To make sure that American interests were protected, the U.S. Government insisted that the new constitution define the relationship between the U.S. and Cuba.

These conditions led to the passing of the Platt Amendment. Under this, Cuba could not make treaties or alliances with other countries; it had to allow U.S. military bases on the island; and it had to agree that the U.S. could intervene on the island in times of crisis. The U.S. Government refused to pull troops from Cuba until these conditions were met, so the Platt Amendment was placed in the Cuban constitution. After a great deal of opposition and debate, the amendment was passed by a margin of one vote. Many Cubans resented the amendment. They saw it as an assault on their independence. Anti-American feelings swept Cuba. U.S. troops left Cuba in 1902.

Hague Peace Conference

Countries around the world were scrambling to get their hands on more military arms. In 1907, some countries were allotting up to 6 percent of their national income for the military. This was an incredible ratio in times of peace. On June 15, 1907, representatives of forty-four countries came together in The Hague, Netherlands, for a four-month meeting. They wanted to discuss disarming the world.

This was the Second Hague Peace Conference—the first had been held in 1899 and had established international laws and set guidelines for war. The 1907 conference built on what was agreed upon at the first conference. This Second Peace Conference expanded the powers of The Hague court and agreed on the rights and duties of neutral powers in wartime. It also discussed such issues as underwater mines and the practice of converting merchant ships into warships. The building of arms across the globe had prompted this conference, but the issue of disarmament was

■ The U.S. Mission arrives in the Netherlands to attend the Hague Peace Conference.

barely discussed. The representatives recommended that they meet again within seven years. World War I prevented this from happening.

Where Did It Happen?

Match the following events with the locations in which they happened:

1. The location of the World's Fair
2. The chocolate center in the 1900s
3. Carry Nation's starting point
4. Location of the first airplane launch
5. May Sutton's hometown
6. Location of the Roosevelt Dam

7. Site of the Iroquois Fire
8. Location of a major earthquake
9. The capital of the forty-sixth state in the Union
10. *Peter Pan* opened

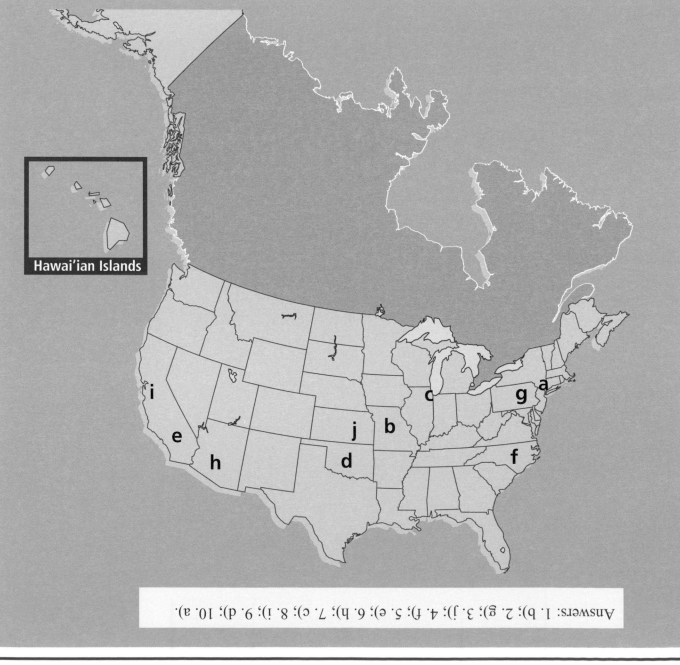

Hawai'ian Islands

Answers: 1. b); 2. g); 3. j); 4. f); 5. e); 6. h); 7. c); 8. i); 9. d); 10. a).

Multiple Choice

Choose the correct answer to the following:

1 President McKinley
a) was due to call an election when he was killed.
b) died immediately after being shot.
c) was the third president to be shot in fifty years.

2 The eruption of Montagne Pelée
a) wiped out St. Pierre.
b) killed about 3,000 people.
c) caused Mt. Etna to erupt.

3 Dr. James Naismith invented
a) motion pictures.
b) basketball.
c) chocolate.

4 Upton Sinclair's novel *The Jungle*
a) led to regulations in meat packing.
b) won the Pulitzer Prize.
c) was about corruption in the newspaper industry.

5 Jack Johnson
a) won the first Noble Prize.
b) was a cubist painter.
c) boxed professionally for twenty-seven years.

Answers: 1. c); 2. a); 3. b); 4. a); 5. c).

Newsmakers

Match the person in the news with his or her claim to fame.

1. novelist

2. first to reach North Pole

3. marathon runner

4. illustrator

5. member of NAACP

6. drew first U.S. cartoon strip

7. famous pitcher

8. wrote many American musicals

9. smashed saloons

10. steel-industry mogul

a) George Cohan
b) Cy Young
c) Carry Nation
d) Robert Peary
e) J. P. Morgan
f) Jack London
g) Rose O'Neill
h) Frank Lorz
i) W. E. B. Du Bois
j) R. F. Outcault

Answers: 1. f); 2. d); 3. h); 4. g); 5. i); 6. j); 7. b); 8. a); 9. c); 10. e).

advocate: support, help promote

anarchist: a person who does not believe in governments

annexation: to take over something and join it to a larger body

bisque: unglazed china

celluloid: a type of plastic

charismatic: a person with great charm and appeal who attracts people to him or her

colonial: connected with a nation's colonies

dictation: speaking aloud so someone can write down or record what is said

exempted: not having to do what others have to do

fluctuate: rise and fall irregularly

guerrilla: fighting done in small groups that are independent of the military

irrigation: watering systems for crops, etc.

isthmus: a narrow strip of land bordered on both sides by water

manifesto: a declaration of intentions or opinions

mediate: act as peacemaker or negotiator

melting pot: a country in which a blending of cultures takes place

pacifist: a person who does not believe in war

patent: an official document giving a person the right to produce and sell a specific design

precedent: a legal decision that serves as an example

prohibition: laws banning the making and sale of alcohol

prospectors: people who explore an area looking for gold and other minerals

provisional: temporary

ragamuffin: a child in dirty and ragged clothing

recession: an extended period of economic decline

revues: shows made up of many different acts, including skits and songs

segregation: keeping people of different races apart

suffrage: the right to vote

sweatshops: places where people work long hours for little pay in poor conditions

three-dimensional: having length, width, and height

Transvaal: a province in South Africa

tsunami: a large wave of water caused by an earthquake

vaudeville: a light theatrical performance of songs and dances

violating: going against the rules

Here are some book resources and Internet links if you want to learn more about the people, places, and events that made headlines during the 1900s.

Books

Brewster, Todd, and Peter Jennings. *The Century for Young People*. New York: Random House, 1999.

Estrin, Jack C. American History Made Simple. New York: The Stonesong Press, 1991.

Howard, Fred. *Wilbur and Orville*. Knopf, New York, 1987.

London, Jack. *The Call of the Wild*. Holt Rinehart and Winston, 1903.

Internet Links

http://www.pbs.org/wgbh/amex/1900/

http://www.scottjoplin.org

http://www.kshs.org/cool2/coolcary.htm

For information about other U.S. subjects, type your key words into a search engine such as Alta Vista or Yahoo!